This book belongs to

_____

It is all about a puppy named

_____

It was started on

_____

Tips for using this book

Only use glue that is suitable for paper (such as a glue stick) when pasting photos in this book. For collages and other special arrangements, first mount the photos in the desired position onto a strong piece of paper cut slightly smaller than the page size of this book. Once dry, carefully glue the sheet (with photos attached) into the book.

My Puppy's
Baby Book

A Special Book of Puppy Memories and Milestones

A Brolly Book

Place a puppy photograph here.

I was born...

The date
_____

[insert approximate date if actual date not known]

The place
_____

[insert approximate place if actual date not known]

My gender
_____

My breed
_____

Other things about me at this time
_____

_____

I came home to my people family...

On
_____

To
_____

My people family named me
_____

Because
_____

Other special things about me
_____

_____

When I came home ...

My fur was

[describe fur: long, short, curly, soft, wiry, the colour, etc.]

The colour of my eyes was

My ears were

[describe ears: long, short, silky, upright, pointy, round, etc.]

The length of my body was

[measure from the base of the tail to the 'withers', the highest point of the shoulders]

My height was

[measure from ground to withers]

My entire length from the tip of my nose to the tip of my tail

[always measure gently and carefully and if your puppy does not want you to, stop immediately!]

My weight was

Friends and family

People in my animal family

_____

_____

Animals in my animal family

_____

_____

Use this page for photographs

My favourite things

Food
_____

Toys
_____

Games
_____

Time of day _____ because _____

_____

My favourite things

Place to play

Place to walk

Place to sit

Place to sleep

Favourite photos

My first friends

My first friends were
_____

I met them at
_____

Things I did with my first friends
_____

_____

The first time I...

Had a bath

Went for a walk

Did something on command

When I . . .

[for example, sat down on command]

Went to the vet

Barked

And . . .

[for example, went to puppy school, went on holiday, and the date]

More Favourite Photos

Mischief that I got up to

Things that I did . . .

_____

_____

_____

_____

_____

_____

_____

_____

Special events and adventures

Things I did and saw . . .

_____

_____

_____

_____

_____

_____

Me and my moods

When I am happy I . . .

_____

When I am sad I . . .

_____

When I am cross I . . .

_____

When I am excited I . . .

_____

When I am tired I . . .

_____

When I am hungry I . . .

_____

When I want your attention I . . .

_____

A Pocket full of Memories

The perfect place for
locks of fur, special photos, journal notes,
letters and cards to your puppy, small mementoes
such as name tags, certificates, family tree and breeding notes,
and more. Slip them in here for safe-keeping, and be sure to
individually bag and label them if
you need to first.

Place a favourite photograph here